LIVING TO LEAVE A
LEGACY

KELLY J. NORMAN

Living to Leave a Legacy

Kelly J. Norman

Living to Leave a Legacy© 2018 Kelly J. Norman

Publisher: Kelly J. Norman

P O Box 82, Springer, OK 73458

www.kellyjnorman.com

ISBN: 978-0-692-05781-0

Endorsements

Kelly helped propel me into my God-given destiny. The love and light she shared about loving myself started a paradigm shift in me. I did not even know what that phrase "paradigm shift" meant until she entered my life.

Kelly has been a divine force in my life. My influence among other women has been strengthened because she empowered me. I am eager to watch what Kelly will do next and what they will teach me and so many other women.

Jessie Reagan

Personal happiness? Feeling complete? Forgiveness? Are you challenged by any of these issues in your life? I can guarantee you that Kelly Norman will give you the opportunity to address all of these issues and move on with your life, just as it has with my own. Being able to face each day and live life to the fullest are some of the ways I benefited by investing the time to take part in this amazing workshop. Thanks to Kelly, I can now leave a legacy for my family!

Charlene Newell

I have been eagerly awaiting the arrival of Kelly Norman's new book, *Living to Leave a Legacy*. If you have ever been blessed enough to spend time with this amazing woman of God, then I am sure you are as excited about it as I am to have this book in your hands! She has a gift of lifting up and inspiring people to be fearless and courageous. Kelly has given me a longing to walk closer with Jesus and be empowered by the Holy Spirit. I would encourage you to attend her workshop, join her mentorship program, and buy extra copies of this book to share with those you love.

Jenny Zant

Kelly Norman's trainings have been life-changing. Her honesty and vulnerability make her teachings and trainings so accessible and REAL for everyone who attends. Every aspect applies to life and the relationships you have with your spouse, children, siblings, friends, co-workers, and even God. Through her trainings, I have found the courage to share my personal truth with the world. To me, that is priceless. I would not have been able to do that without Kelly's training.

Andreya Drury

You will find more great endorsements and testimonials at the end of this book.

Dedication

I want to dedicate this book to the woman who has empowered me with a life-changing legacy; one of kindness, love, strength, and grace. She taught me that everyone has good in them; sometimes, you just have to look a little harder to find it! This woman saw the good in me when I could not, and unconditionally loved me through my rebellious years. I dedicate this book to my mother, Lenora Rose Miller. Thank you for not preaching, but rather showing me the heart of God. May others be touched through this book because you chose to show up every day and love your family so well.

Acknowledgments

The pages you are about to read would never have been written had it not been for the people mentioned here. I am truly honored and humbled to be surrounded with such supportive individuals that have believed in me.

To my husband, Buddy, who knows me better than I know myself. I love you with every fiber of my being. Thank you for constantly asking me, "Did you write today?" when you knew I had not. Even when I lost the belief to finish, you believed for me. Thank you for consistently and unconditionally loving me every day of our lives together. God knew I needed you on this beautiful journey!

To my sons, Brady and Blue, thank you for always encouraging me to pursue my dreams, and for all your patience and kindness toward me. May you always know and feel that you and your father are my top priorities. I know each of you are going to do great things that will impact the world!

To my sister, Tammy, thank you for sharing me, for giving up our precious time together so I could write, and for supporting me when it meant a sacrifice for you. I would not be who I am today had it not been for your example and love.

Thank you to the team of T&E Joint Ventures Professional Editing and Publishing for making my book a priority, for your suggestions, and your guidance as I ventured into new territory. You are a gift from God!

Last but definitely not least, I want to thank my heavenly Father. Thank you for Jesus and the Holy Spirit that You lavishly gifted to me, and for healing my soul and allowing me to bravely share and give pieces of my heart away in this book. May Your light shine through the words of this book and heal those who read it.

Table of Contents

Foreword

I have known Kelly for a few years now and am passionate about telling you why you are going to love her book. She is a kind, loving, and passionate woman who thrives on pouring belief into others. Kelly is high on life, has so many lessons of her own to inspire from, and has the biggest heart for inspiring change in others of anyone I know. The love and adoration she has for her family are among the things I love the most about her. She has taught me so much about setting boundaries and forgiveness. I cannot imagine not having her in my life.

I have been self-employed and serving people for almost three decades. My expertise is mindset and overcoming fear. If people do not get their minds fixed, they will always continue to struggle with the answers. As a leader in my company, as a John Maxwell coach, and having worked with Kelly, I can tell you, she has what it takes to create permanent change in people's hearts and minds. They will forever be changed from reading this transforming book with practical and simple application techniques that can lead to a permanent change.

I hope you enjoy this book as much as I have!!!

Sonya Dudley
Certified John Maxwell Coach

Introduction

For years I knew I was to write a book, but the task seemed so big. Anyway, what in the world would I even write about? Then, one day, it became so clear.

A few years ago, I was asked and agreed to speak at a leadership training. I spent three days speaking on leadership and mindset. I was then asked to make some closing remarks at the conclusion of the leadership training event. As I was making my closing remarks, a still soft voice inside of me instructed me to ask the men and women in the audience the following question, "Who speaks positive words over your children?" Every hand in the room was raised! Then I asked, "Who speaks positive words over themselves?" Only two hands went up. At that moment, I heard the still soft voice on the inside of me speaking again. "Kelly, you are being sent out to set others free; free from self-sabotaging ways and wrong mindsets that stand in the way of loving themselves and fulfilling their destiny." This was my Aha moment and the start of my journey to help set others free.

Along this life journey, I have found myself asking that same question to groups of people everywhere I go and, time after time, I experience the same staggering results. With each time I asked that question of others, I heard the still soft voice inside of me gently urging me to finish my book.

So, here it is; a book that is the result of blood, sweat, and tears; a book of vulnerability, honesty (I know no other way), empowerment, simple application, and hopefully, encouragement. It is my desire to instill in each of you a new-found passion and desire to find your freedom and run your race; to fulfill your destiny, and leave a legacy that impacts others.

Several years ago, I would have been the woman that did not raise her hand; but, through my journey of transformation, I am now on the other side. I can confidently say, "I love myself!" Ha, you may say, that sounds haughty. I say no, that sounds whole! I believe it is just perfectly the way we were created to be. I like to call this Freedom; free to be me, to love me, and to step into my destiny; to know my identity, and take others on this journey with me.

So, here I am on my mission to be the vessel and offer you, men and women alike, a few tools that will set you free! Buckle up my friends and enjoy the ride. Our destination is right ahead. Destination Freedom.

Part One

The world is waiting for you!
It's time you step into
what you were created for.
The world needs you.
And it needs you whole.

Chapter 1

The Roller Coaster

I have determined throughout this book that I will be nothing but vulnerable, authentic, and honest with you about my personal journey. So, let's talk about my own journey to freedom.

It all started at a simple stop light. This was such a pivotal moment in my life. So much so that I remember the exact location of the stop light, and exactly what I was driving; a blue Ford Explorer. It was at this stop light when I called out to God. My life was a roller coaster!

You see, I got married at the age of twenty to my soulmate, the most wonderful man in the world; a godly man who has loved me unconditionally every day of our marriage. We met when I was eighteen, with my nineteenth birthday quickly approaching, and he was thiry-one. I had just come back from my first semester of college with every last penny I had in the gas tank of my 1989

LeBaron convertible. When we met, I was a wreck. I was insecure, wounded, and battling many negative voices; all wrapped up in a cute little 120-pound package who had learned the art of survival, and manipulation. I knew how to get what I wanted, especially when it came to a man. All of this equals "dangerous!"

We met, fell in love, and married a year and a half later. Although our love for each other stayed strong, life was hard. You see, I had not yet learned to capture the squatters. To be honest, I did not even know I had any. Webster's online dictionary defines a squatter as "a person who unlawfully occupies an uninhabited building or unused land. A settler with no legal title to the land occupied." These "squatters" that I am talking about are the negative thoughts, the accusing voices that occupy real estate inside our heads. I personally had no idea that the negative thoughts were there unlawfully, and definitely did not know why I was so unstable.

I was tormented by the negative voices daily. Accusations, past failures, and my poor choices played like a slide show inside my head. Life for me was a roller coaster; up one day, and down the next. The situation at hand was that my husband had been married before and already had two children. I was an 18-year-old broken woman with an identity crisis.

Picture this: My husband, my husband's ex-wife, two children, and me; an outspoken, opinionated, insecure, mentally, and emotionally unstable woman. That mixes like vinegar and oil. I think you get the picture. Back to God at the stop light.

My mother had raised me in church and loved God with all her heart. She had modeled stability and taught me that God was faithful. Because of her example, I cried out to God. "God, I am like a roller coaster! Up high one day, and down low the next. There has to be more to this life."

In church, I had heard sermons about Jesus, how He died on the cross for me, and provided peace for those that believed. At the age of 11, I became a Christian. I had attended Sunday School and church every time the door was open. I had heard Jesus described as the Prince of Peace but I certainly was not experiencing any peace.

My heart was broken for the people in my life because I knew how toxic it must have been to be around me. After crying out to God, I heard His voice for the first time in my life! It was not audible, but it was just as real as an audible voice. He said, "I am the same yesterday, today, and tomorrow. Imitate Me!" Those words echoed through my soul. Little did I know at the time that those words were actually scriptures in the Bible.

Something in me said, "Say it." So, I did. I said, "I am the same every day. I am the same yesterday, today, and tomorrow." I said it for what seemed like one hundred times a day. I wrote it everywhere I looked; in journals, on my bathroom mirror, in my car. Just those few words spoken out loud everyday started a radical transformation. You see, the negative thoughts said I was

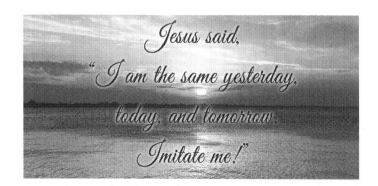

unstable; I was a roller coaster. But, that was not my destiny. That was not who I was created to be. The seed of virtue was within me and I started to hear this seed whispering the truth. I started to believe I was created to be the same every day; stable, unwavering.

My friends, what are the accusing voices telling you? Do you identify with my story and hear things like, "You are unstable?" Maybe they say, "You always fail. You're ugly. You're awkward. No one wants to listen to you." I am here to help you expose the squatters that have settled in your land and replace them with the truth. Truths like, "You are beautifully and wonderfully made. You are a success and a conqueror. You have a unique voice that the world needs to hear!" You are that beautiful apple tree that is planted by streams of water and destined to bear much fruit! The seed is within you!

Through this book, you are going to be given the tools to awaken that seed and step into your truth. You, my friend, are going to learn the power in replacing the lies with speaking the truth! I cannot wait for you to put words to the seed of success that is within you; to replace EVERY negative thought with the truth.

Chapter 2

The Mirror

Little girls and boys all love mirrors. Ladies, can you recall putting your mom's make-up on and dressing up like a princess? You would put your little feet in her high heels and dance in front of the mirror, dreaming of your fairytale future. This future that you were dreaming of as you stood in front of the mirror may have included a beautiful palace, prince charming, wonderful food, music, dancing, and lots of laughter. One thing was for sure, you were beautiful! Oh, how the mirror was a place to dream and see yourself as a princess. Maybe you had one of those hand-held mirrors with pink ceramic around it, or maybe you had to stand on the counter to see your whole self in that radiant beauty. Maybe you were lucky enough to have a full-length mirror that you could see yourself in from head to toe and dance all around. Those were the days! Dreaming, dancing, and feeling beautiful!

Guys, perhaps you recall standing in front of the mirror seeing yoursef hitting that home run, making the game winning pass, riding that eight second bull. I would dare to say you fought and won many brave battles with your imaginary sword in the mirror. You often reveled at your shiny armor and all of its courageous fullness. This sword you held up before your image in the mirror was not like any other. It was bright and heavy. Most men could not carry it; but, you could, because you were the strongest of all. You were the courageous knight, the mighty warrior that led others into war. Single handedly you saved the beautiful princess time and time again.

Oh, how the mirror was a place to dream and see yourself as a princess, or a conqueror! Those were the days. Ladies, dreaming, dancing and feeling beautiful. Gentlemen, imagining yourself as that victorious warrior and experienced conqueror.

Then, one day, it slowly started to happen. The voices came! Voices that, little by little, started to rob you of your fairytale dreams and your mighty exploits of valor; robbed you of your destiny, and your identity. You did not realize what was happening because it all came so slowly until one day you looked in the mirror, and there was no trace of that beautiful princess or conquering hero anymore. Your beauty had been replaced with ugly, and your shiny sword replaced with a shovel.

Although the stories might be a bit different, they all lead to the same question, "How did this happen?"

You can remember dreaming like it was yesterday. Those vague memories of childlike wonder:

seeing life in brilliant colors,

feeling excitement for your future,

and knowing who you were.

Ladies, you felt so beautiful when you looked in the mirror and applied that shimmery lip gloss. You can even remember that sweet smell of the strawberry scent. Gentlemen, you were feeling strong as you gazed at your image. You securely tied the belt around your waist to hold the sword before going into battle.

Fast forward 20 or 40 years and all the color seems to have faded. You now see life in black and white rather than in vibrant and brilliant colors. The mirror is the last place you want to look, and that future you were so excited about has faded into disappointments, failures, and regrets.

The voices you now hear are telling you that you are not smart enough, strong enough, skinny enough, pretty enough, or handsome enough. You are too tall, or too short, you don't have the right personality, you are too weak, too strong, not nice enough, you are too nice, and you are certainly not wealthy enough. They even say you will certainly never be successful, so why even try?

These voices begin to take on a personality of their own and have the nerve to suggest that people just tolerate you and do not really like you. The suggestions from the voices become a litany of statements that begin to consume you as they thunder in your mind. They shout accusations and remind you of all your past failures, rejections, and poor choices. They remind you of when you made that horrible decision that nobody knows about, or the one that everyone knows about. They transport you to the place where you believe you have failed as a mom, dad, husband, wife, sister, brother, son, daughter, friend, businessman, or businesswoman.

Then, all of a sudden, guilt sweeps over you. The voices are like recordings that play over and over and you cannot seem to stop them. You hate the mirror! Looking in it makes you think the voices are true. You feel so unworthy of being loved by anyone, much less being able to love yourself.

If this is you, then I want you to know, you are not alone. Men and women across the planet are silently suffering from listening to "the voices." My dear friend, you have picked up this book by divine appointment. I am so excited to tell you that I have good news. You, yes you, have a choice and can be set free! Set free from insecurity, guilt, condemnation and what I like to call the lying voices that have not only eroded but completely stolen your very identity. I dare to say that, if you will commit to finishing this book and applying the principles within it, you will start to see life in color again, and start to love the one you see in the mirror.

Chapter 3

Spectators of Life

Mary and John were dreamers. From the moment they woke up, they loved to pretend and dream all day. They were wide-eyed at the world, and caught up in its wonder! Although they were from different parts of the world, different families, and different cultures, their stories intertwine.

Mary loved to admire beautiful butterflies. John loved to catch lightning bugs on warm summer nights. Both of them loved to collect special rocks and pretend being on many wonderful adventures. They found joy in animals, their siblings, and little friends next door! They were happy, loved life, and had big dreams of doing great things.

Both of them saw their parents as rich and able to provide for the desires of their hearts. The day finally came for Mary and John to go to school. They were so excited that they spent hours picking out the perfect outfit; Mary chose the most beautiful dress she owned, and John picked out his favorite pants and matching shirt. They were very bright, learned quickly, and loved the chocolate milk. The teachers loved Mary for her sweet spirit, and John for his eagerness to serve and learn.

Several years went by. Mary's and John's parents both experienced financial hardship. Mary had to change schools several times only to sadly find out that it was quite hard for the new kid to fit in. John also found himself being bullied and mocked. Mary discovered that she didn't have the right clothes and was never invited to all the social events. John was never invited to just hang out with the guys. Kindness only went so far in the rough world of elementary and middle school. Girls could be mean, guys could be cruel, and the words and rejection from both of their peers hurt more than they knew.

On top of rejection at school, the hardships at home caused their fathers to become emotionally abusive. As children, the hurtful words and rejection penetrated their young hearts and brought shame to both of them.

Sadly, compounding the wounded hearts, it was not long before their innocence was violated and invaded.

Before long, Mary and John started to believe the lies that others spoke over them and accepted the shame that became part of who they were. Both now found themselves as spectators of life; watching others have fun, seeing the dreams of others being fulfilled, and never really feeling worthy of happiness themselves. Those big dreams they both had were now just a vague memory.

From the outside, nobody knew Mary and John always felt empty and alone. Both of them kept their insecurities to themselves. One day, they started to look toward other things to fill the void. Both ended up hanging out with the wrong crowd which was where they felt accepted. They began to make choices they thought they would never make.

The voices that had started when Mary and John were young had now bedded down deep inside their souls, made themselves at home, and pretended that's where they belonged. Now, as adults, when they each look in the mirror, the voices still talk and replay all the hurtful words from their peers and their own father, accusing them of being filthy, unfit, and unworthy of love.

Some days Mary and John have a faint recollection of their youthful brilliance and innocent wonder, but it is quickly stolen by the voices that produce emotions of failure, guilt, shame, and rejection. The voices even affect their marriages. Even though their spouses love them dearly, they are not capable of being loved or of trusting another human being. They feel unworthy and of no value. The voices have caused both Mary and John to build walls that no one can get past. They have become cold, untrusting, and controlling, always correcting their spouses and never meeting their needs. They now feel disrespected, unloved, and have no confidence of their own.

Truth be told, both have thoughts of infidelity, feeling that the attention from another will make them feel wanted and valuable again.

Mary and John have isolated themselves from any friendships in order to avoid more rejection and hurt. Both often feel lonely but prefer to stay behind the big but illusive wall of emotional safety. Their youth, adulthood, marriages, relationships, and dreams have been stolen by the negative voices. Many times,

Mary wonders where the beautiful princess went; John wonders whatever happened to the conquering hero.

Although your story might be somewhat different than Mary's or John's, I would bet you have asked yourself the same question, "How did I get here?" Perhaps your story involves losing someone you loved, or watching your parents navigate the rough waters of a painful divorce. Perhaps you were sexually abused. Perhaps you found yourself abandoned in a relationship, or held bondage to an addiction. No matter the form of your abuse or hardship, you can probably identify with the question, "How did I get here?" So many of us wake up feeling that life has just dumped us out and that our dreams are just that, dreams of the past left unfulfilled.

Chapter 4

Neuroplasticity

What if I told you that you can dream again, that you can see life once again in full color? You can be free? You can rid yourself of the negative or accusing voices and tear down those walls? What if I told you that you can replace them? You can be rewired? Your negative, accusing thoughts can be traded out with thoughts that encourage, empower, and cheer you on? You can go from being your own worst enemy to your own biggest encourager; your biggest fan?

You, my friend, can renew your mind, change your life, and fall in love with yourself again! Your brain can be rewired. This is called neuroplasticity. Neuroplasticity is the brain's ability to reorganize itself by forming new neural connections throughout life, especially in response to learning, or experience, or following an injury.

Now, don't worry. This book you are reading is not full of scientific terms. I am a pretty simple woman and like to teach and share on basic terms and principles that we can all understand. With that out of the way, let's resume.

You possess everything it takes to change the way you think, which in turn will change your life. With just a flip of the switch and some daily discipline you can take back your life. If you will commit to reading this book and completing the exercises that I recommend, I believe you will find yourself regaining what was once stolen from you: Purity, Adventure, Joy, Peace, Love, Wonder, Value, Dreams and, most importantly, Hope. Not only will you regain these valuable possessions, but you will once again love the one in the mirror!

I believe there are things on this earth that only you can do; things that were created long before you were even born. You have purpose, you have a call, and you have a date with destiny. Time is ticking. Great and marvelous works were divinely created and designed for you before your life on earth began. We must get you on your flight that soars to freedom and starts you on your way to discovering the perfection within, and to fulfilling your unique purpose and calling. The world is waiting for you to discover your inner strength and beauty. It's time you step into what you were created for. The world needs you, and it needs you whole.

The world is waiting for you! It's time you step into what you were created for.

Chapter 5

Where do I start?

As you are reading this you may say, "Kelly, this sounds all fine and well. I earnestly desire this wholeness and freedom you talk about, but where do I start?"

I am so glad you asked! Let's take a second and talk about starting. Such a simple word that carries so much power.

I have come to the realization that in my struggles (insecurity, comparison, condemnation) I become paralyzed. When I find myself in this paralyzed state, starting does not even seem like a possible option. If I were a betting woman, I would say you are overwhelmed mentally and physically and can identify with those feelings of being paralyzed at times. You can identify with the hardship of starting. This book will be just what you need to feel energized and equipped to get up! Not only get up, but to get started, and take that action. So, what do you say? Let's take another look in the mirror, and decide to start seeing yourself as valuable and worthy.

If you say, "Kelly, I can't see it. I don't see value and worth when I look at myself," then do this, just remind yourself of all the people that are counting on you; the people close to you that you love. Maybe it's little eyes looking up to you, a teenager lost in this world, a spouse that longs for how it used to be, or an aging parent that needs you. Thinking of them alone should cause your insides to stir and give you what it takes to start this journey; to do whatever it takes to get to a place of loving the one in the mirror.

I can only speak from my own experiences and how I began. I believe a good starting place for your own journey is to take a look at your thoughts. Let's think about what we are thinking about.

The average person thinks 30,000 to 50,000 thoughts a day! Wow, that is a lot of thoughts in one day. For years I believed the 50,000 referred to women, and the 30,000 referred to men. I have come to this revolutionary conclusion from taking long trips in the car with my husband. Looking over and asking the one big question that many of us women have asked, "What are you thinking?" I quickly saw the deer in the headlights look and heard the response, "Nothing." I proceeded to ask him, "Can a man actually think nothing?" He answered with a reassuring, "Yes." Hmm, was it true? Can a man, unlike a woman, think nothing? Or could it be that maybe it is harder for a man to talk about his thoughts and feelings so freely and openly on the spot? Perhaps that is for a later book, but right now we can establish that all of us are thinking a lot of thoughts throughout the course of our day.

Taking a look at how many thoughts we think a day is very important, because it has been discovered that your thoughts determine your beliefs and feelings. Your beliefs and feelings then direct your actions. Your actions are your world, your life, the results that you see and experience each and every day. Norman Vincent Peale, minister and author of The Power of Positive Thinking, says, "Change your thoughts and you change your world." Norman's teachings are among the forerunners of the power of the mind.

In the mid-1900s scientists, and even the church, refused his teachings; but, they have since come around to the idea that our thoughts truly do dictate our life. Scientist Dr. Caroline Leaf says, "75-98% of mental, physical and behavioral illnesses come from toxic thinking." I once heard a man say, "I would rather eat unhealthy and think positively than eat broccoli and think toxic thoughts." I do not know how proven that statement is, but it caught my attention. Can it be true? Can toxic thinking release toxins in your body that make you sick? From my research and experience I would say the answer is a resounding yes! Researchers have even said depression has been connected with an increased risk for type 2 diabetes, heart attack, and a greater chance of disability later in life.

Now that we have established the physical importance of our thought life, let's take a deeper look into how the thoughts are established, and how they can affect our lives emotionally.

Earlier I talked about the negative or accusing voices. You have probably figured out by now that the negative or accusing voices I refer to are our thoughts. Some of you reading this book are being tormented daily by your very own negative or accusing thoughts. Wow, such a revelation. We are holding ourselves in bondage and, worse than that, we are torturing ourselves! Many of us thought our pain was someone or something else's fault. But, the fact of the matter is, we are responsible for ourselves. Now, don't throw the book across the room or get mad at me. I am not saying what someone else did to you is acceptable. I am saying that life is 10% of what happens to us, and 90% of what we do with it.

Stay with me and give me a chance. Perhaps I have something that can help you.

Behind every one of these negative tormenting voices (which we have now established are our thoughts) are lies or beliefs that are simply not true. A wise old man once told me, "Any thought that doesn't shimmer with hope in your life is an indicator that you are believing a lie."

Before we continue, answer the following question:

"What areas in your life are not shimmering with hope?"

1. _____

2. _____

3. _____

4. _____

5. _____

PART TWO

*You cannot change your past,
but you can certainly rewrite it.
Bring a new and fresh perspective
to the events that shaped your life.*

Chapter 6

Programming

*I*f you are like me, you have a few questions. Questions like, "Where did all these thoughts come from? How did I get here?" I would like to enlighten you on the fact that the thoughts you and I think are results of our programming. You see, your brain is programmed like a computer. For instance, if I typed, "Kelly is clumsy," my computer would not say, "Kelly, you are not clumsy!" No, you and I both know it would take the information in as a fact. Thus, the same with your brain. When I tell myself, or unconsciously take in what others say about me, statements such as, "I am clumsy," my brain receives this information as factual.

This programming started before we could even walk. It is what we were told by others, what we told ourselves, the people we hang around with, the books we read, the movies and television shows we've watched. Studies show that by the time a child finishes elementary school, the number of murders seen on TV is about 8,000. The fact of the matter is, you and I had no choice regarding adolescent and childhood programming because we had no control of what we were exposed to by our parents.

Studies further show that our brains are 85% developed by the age of eight. Wow! BUT, do not let that discourage you. There is good news. You and I now have choices, and we just learned a new powerful word, "Neuroplasticity." You and I can choose to rewire our brains! We can choose what thoughts are welcome to stay, and what thoughts we need to throw out and replace with positive thoughts. Today, I am proud to say, I control my thoughts, my thoughts do not control me, and you can do the same thing, too. Are you ready to go a bit deeper?

Science has proven that our minds were created for love, for positivity. So, any thought that is not based on faith, truth, and love causes confusion and, left alone, can create walls of lies that build strong towers in your mind. You may have heard these walls described as strongholds. Scientist, author, and speaker, Dr. Caroline Leaf, (mentioned above) refers to these thoughts as dead trees. This is because, when a picture is taken of the brain while thinking a negative thought, you will see an image that looks like dead trees. These dead trees produce chemicals in the body that we call downers. The downers cause feelings of despair and depression. This despair and depression result in the killing of shimmering hope, a valuable ingredient that is so necessary to fuel us on our journey of dreaming and feel energized to take action. The downers can even cause illness in our body, thus leaving you hopeless and sick.

Let's take a look at Mary and John again. In their earlier school days when they were rejected by their peers, the thoughts of not being good enough crept in. Mary and John both innocently took these lying thoughts as truth. Dead trees started forming, and walls began to be erected. Then, as they grew older and their fathers spoke words of destruction over them, the trees became a forest, and the walls just got stronger and stronger thus creating a stronghold; a tower in Mary's and John's minds that held them captive. All hope was lost, and they now believed that the rejection and lying words defined them. (A prime example that our thoughts direct our beliefs!)

Each had a tower of destruction built on lies. They had no value or self-worth, which in turn caused their actions to line up with this fabrication. Mary and John grew into young adults who did not expect others to treat them with value because they did not see themselves as valuable. The choices and actions both of them made were from a place of insecurity and unworthiness. They became people whose emotions were as a roller coaster; down one minute, and up another.

Each of them felt that they had a reason to blame their roller coaster life solely on hormones. I am not saying hormones do not affect our moods but, when we can take a holistic approach which includes body, soul, and spirit, we see that many times, we can be guilty of only putting a bandage on this issue, or only partly addressing a problem. Possibly, if we take a little deeper look into the root cause of these ups and downs, we might find the biggest culprit; the lying voices/thoughts that have set up a camp in our heads.

What about you? Are you up one day and down another? Do you feel like your mind is a run-away train that you cannot stop? Do you have feelings of regret, unworthiness, shame, and rejection? This usually starts from our childhood experiences and programming. This programming filters the way we see life, thus causing more lies to form. An example of this would be someone who innocently did or said something that they did not mean as bad but, because you filtered the words or actions through your programming, you are offended. The saying, "Sticks and stones may break my bones but words will never harm me," is a catchy saying but totally untrue! Those hurtful words of the past turn into sticks and stones that build fortresses to hold us captive inside our own heads. These fortresses manufacture toxic hormones and we start to self-destruct emotionally and physically.

But wait! I want to remind you of the good news!! You have a choice. You can choose today to START; start your journey to setting yourself free.

ACTIVATION

Part 1 – Your Assignment

Take a blank sheet of paper and write down every negative thought you think. Every lie you have believed. For starters, you may identify with a number of the following.

You are:

- not smart enough,
- skinny enough,
- pretty enough,
- handsome enough,
- strong enough.

You:

- are too tall,
- too short,
- do not have the right personality,
- are too weak,
- too strong,
- are socially awkward,
- not a leader,
- not nice enough,

- too nice.
- You cannot be successful.
- People do not like you.
- No one wants to hear what you have to say.
- You are not organized.
- You are clumsy.
- You are addicted to _____.
- You cannot diet,
- cannot lose weight,
- cannot lift weights,
- are not disciplined.
- Your past failures dictate your future.
- Everyone else can be free and whole but not you,
- and all the other lies that you have received as truth.

My biggest advice to you is to take time for this; DO NOT HURRY through it. I encourage you to find a comfortable chair, get a cup of hot tea or coffee, relax, and choose a time when you can be all alone. Before you know it, you will surprisingly find a page full of untruths that you have been believing about yourself.

You may ask, "Kelly, how do you know this?" Well, the answer is, I know from first-hand experience. You are talking to someone who was imprisoned by the same lies; one who has been redeemed and set free from the lying voices. The good news is, you are headed on the path to your destination of freedom, too! Do not forget that not only are you worth it, but there are others who are counting on you to be whole. Your family, friends, your circle of influence all need you whole. Spend your time on this valuable exercise that will be the start to your breakthrough and, once you are done, move on to part 2.

Throwing out the Squatters

Congrats on finishing that last exercise! You, my friend, have just identified and captured what I like to call "the squatters."

As I stated earlier, your mind was not made for the lies, and the squatters have no right to be there. Therefore, they are trespassing! You were created to house the truth; the rightful occupants to your land. Once again, congratulations. You have taken the first step towards freedom. BUT, it is with great caution that I tell you, "DO NOT STOP HERE!" These squatters must be thrown out and REPLACED with positive occupants.

Did you notice in the definition of *squatter* the words "unused land?" If you leave the land of your mind unoccupied, these squatters will return with a vengeance. That is why you must intentionally occupy your mind with the truth.

Let me give you an example: Let's suppose I was your neighbor and one morning you called me and told me with great excitement that you were going to purchase fabulous new furniture for your entire house. You then asked if I could help you move the old furniture out. I eagerly came over and we moved all the old furniture out to the garage. After a full day of moving you said, "Kelly, let's call it a day. I am tired." I agreed to your suggestion to quit the project, thinking that the next day you would feel like buying the new furniture that would replace the old. But you didn't. And with each new day, things pop up and you never get around to buying your new furniture. That first night, when suppertime came around, the kids cried out for a chair to sit in. So, you thought, *What's the big deal? I will just bring a few chairs back in.* Then you discover that your spouse is not a fan of sleeping on the floor so the next day, when nighttime rolls around, you drag a mattress back in. One piece of old furniture at a time comes back in and, before you know it, all the old furniture is right back in the house where it started from.

The moral of this story is, you have to replace the negative thoughts with the positive thoughts or the old negative thoughts will come back! You have to replace the lies with the truth or you will go back to what is familiar. I cannot emphasize enough; it is not sufficient to just identify and capture the lying voices. You must replace them.

ACTIVATION

Part 2 – Your Assignment

Replacing Negative Thoughts with Truth

Now get a NEW piece of paper out and start replacing every negative thought with the truth. Do not skip any negative thoughts. Take time to thoughtfully write out your truths. See the negative thoughts vanish in a bubble cloud above your head as you write out the truths.

I think this is a great time for a time out! Some of you are getting overwhelmed. You might be having a hard time writing down the "truth." Maybe thoughts of unworthiness are creeping in and you disqualify yourself by saying, "That's for people like you. That is not me." What I am about to tell you next will set you free from the paralyzing feelings you might be experiencing right now.

Personal Notes and Insights

_____

_____

_____

_____

_____

_____

_____

_____

_____

_____

_____

_____

_____

_____

_____

_____

_____

_____

_____

_____

_____

_____

_____

_____

Chapter 7

The Seed of Greatness Is Within You

*I*s the apple tree called an apple tree before or after it bears fruit? You are right, of course – before! Why? Because the apple tree was destined to bear the fruit; the seed of the apple was within it.

My friends, do not believe the negative thoughts. Do not believe that you are writing things that do not reflect you. You are destined to bear the fruit! The seed of perfection and greatness is within you. Just because you do not see it does not mean that is not who you are. I believe you and I are called, destined, and created to be men and women of valor and virtue.

It is interesting that when you look at the Greek word for valor and virtuous you will find it is the same word: *arete*. In other words, when we look at the meaning of *arete*, we discover that you and I are enough. We are courageous, worthy, able, and strong.

One of my favorite stories is about a man named Gideon. Gideon was an Israelite and, during his lifetime, his people had abandoned God. This left them under the oppression of the Midianites. The Midianites would ravenously pass through the Israelites' village and plunder it bare, leaving them without food, drink, and livestock.

In this story, we find Gideon hiding out under a tree making wine for himself and his people. When an angel of God came to Gideon he stated, (paraphrased), "God is with you, you mighty man of valor! God sees you as one of His mightiest warriors!" I picture Gideon looking around to see who this angel is talking to. Surely someone great was standing not far from him. Gideon just knew it could not possibly be himself.

Gideon soon figured out that he was exactly the one the angel was talking to. He might have said something like, "Dude, I'm sorry but you have to be confusing me with a different man. I am from the least of the clans, and I am the least of them." In other words, "Me? A warrior? Ha! I am a nobody from a family of nobodies. A warrior? Ha! I have retreated, hidden, and failed more times than you can imagine. God doesn't want to use a failing nobody like me!"

But, God saw a mighty warrior when Gideon saw a lowly nobody. Thankfully, Gideon trusted what God saw and obeyed. Gideon raised up a small army to defeat the large enemy that had been oppressing them. The Israelites lived in freedom as long as Gideon was alive.

You can find this remarkable story in Judges chapter 6 in your Bible.

How about it? How can you identify with Gideon?

_____

_____

_____

_____

_____

_____

_____

_____

Do you feel like a nobody that is hiding in fear? _____

If so, I hope you will let this story encourage you. There are so many more good things in you than what you see!

ACTIVATION

Assignment 1

Burn the lies

On your new sheet of paper, you are replacing every negative thought with the truth. See the lies vanish in your mind's eye, and then burn the original paper with all the old lying thoughts! That's right. Set a flame to it, but please don't burn down your house.

Also write out these truths here, to keep a permanent record of them:

_____

_____

_____

_____

_____

_____

_____

_____

_____

If you are feeling weak right now, then listen up. You can do this. You are stronger than you think you are. You are worthy, and your destiny is Freedom! Not to mention, you have a lot of people that are counting on you. Some of them you know, and some of them you will encounter in your future. They need you whole.

Congratulations on accomplishing the first step towards your Freedom! I am so proud of you, and I know you must be proud of yourself. Did you know it is ok to be proud of yourself? This may be a new feeling for you, but get used to it. You are going to learn how to celebrate your amazingness through this book and make it your lifestyle, your new habit. Celebration of yourself will begin to be your new normal.

Extra notes and reflections:

_____

_____

_____

_____

_____

_____

_____

_____

_____

_____

_____

How to create healthy new habits

We are going to focus on how to walk out your new freedom every day and also create healthy new habits.

Did you know that your brain is like a muscle? The more you work it, the stronger it gets. So, just like going to the gym one time will not get the results you want, saying your truths once will not either. Today, you must decide this is your new way of speaking and thinking. It takes 21 days to break old mindsets, and two more cycles of 21 to form new ones. That is a total of 63 days. Are you willing to make that commitment to 63 days? I have to be honest with you, most people give up in the first week. Wait, I never said it was easy. I said it was worth it!

Assignment 2

Week One:

Set a time aside every morning, noon, and night to say your new truths; your affirmations. Note: This is done out loud. I know, I know. You feel weird doing it and would rather just say them in your head. What I am about to say, I say with much love and compassion: Get Over It!! You are breaking negative thoughts, stepping out of your comfort zone, and taking back your land. The little bit of being uncomfortable is worth it. Feel that mighty warrior begin to rise up on the inside of you. This warrior has been there all along.

As you go throughout this new journey, there will most likely be a few negative thoughts which will come to the surface that you may have missed. All you will need to do is add the new truth to your affirmations and see the negative thoughts vanish in your head. The exciting part is you will soon start to identify the negative thoughts as they start to form in their infancy. You are now strengthening new keen senses, and healthy habits will start to form. Before long, it will be your automatic reflex to cancel any new negative thoughts that try to sneak in. Picture a trash can in your mind. When a toxic, lying thought pops in your head, stop and say, "That is not the truth," and throw it away in your mind's eye trash can. Then, speak the truth!

Your Gates

When you arrive at week two, you must celebrate yourself once again. You are now one of the few that has beat the odds! You, my friend, have persevered. There is your new truth, "I persevere. I am a finisher." On week two, you will continue with your affirmations three times a day, but this time I want you to add speaking in front of a mirror in one of the sessions. That's right. Look yourself in the eyes and speak the truth!

The next two weeks will consist of continuing your affirmations three times a day. I want to warn you; there may be a few tears involved. This is a powerful part of the process in breaking negative thought. Not only are your ears hearing your voice speak, but now you are seeing the truth with your own eyes. I have heard it said that the eyes are the gateway to the soul. The more of your senses that get involved the better. Think about it. If you and I experience the world and perceive it through all of our five senses: Touch, Taste, Sound, Sight, Smell, don't you think it is a good idea to get as many senses involved as possible?

I like to call our five senses our gates. Our gates are a place where information, experiences, and perception go in and out. Just watch a baby. When they discover something new, the first place it goes is in their mouth. They have to further investigate this new-found discovery. You may not stick everything in your mouth any more, but every day, every second, your senses are taking in more than you can fathom.

If you are changing your life, then you need to be aware of what is going in and out of your gates. Taking it a step further, you need to set a guard outside your gates! (Remember, change your thoughts, change your life.) With this renewing process, you will now be forming an awareness of the need to make a habit of guarding your gates. Soon, you will be very aware of what comes in and goes out of your gates; your eyes, ears and mouth.

Once again, I want to warn you, this new exercise will feel uncomfortable. But, who knows? Maybe a little pride will be broken off, too! Oh, wait. I bet I am the only one that has had issues with pride. It is probably just me. You don't deal with it, right? That was in my sarcastic voice, if you couldn't tell!

We all deal with that sneaky fox. Pride likes to disguise itself as a cute little fox, but, it's the cute little foxes that destroy the whole vine (Song of Solomon 2:15). A long time ago in King Solomon's day they had a lot of vineyards, and the little foxes would gnaw at the roots of the vines. Once the roots were damaged, the vines would start to die and greatly affect the health and production of the fruit. This is such a great illustration of what little things, such as pride, can do to us.

Let's consider what pride might look like in this process.

Pride may say:

- I don't need to add this silly exercise of the mirror. That's for people that have "real issues."
- I bet I can just say my truths for about a week and be good.
- I will just say my affirmations in my head. No one should have to be that uncomfortable.
- I am so busy. Who has time for all this? I have important things to do.

Do not listen to pride. Pride comes in disguise and wants to keep you in walls of imprisonment. Listen to the truth, this new truth you are discovering, and find your inner warrior that is going to push through being uncomfortable and the familiarity of wanting to go back. Do not retreat!

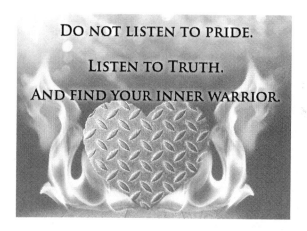

Boundaries

As you are creating new habits in your thoughts, let's take a look at a few other things you might want to change. Many of those lying voices were started by what others have said about and to you; your programming.

As you are on your journey to finding the real authentic you, find that young child that had big dreams, great adventures, and joyous wonder. Take a minute to look around. Look at who you are spending most of your time with. I want to ask you a question, and please be honest, "Do the people in your life agree with you about your old negative thoughts, and do they even add their own negativity and toxic thoughts to the ones that are already in your head?" If so, this is another area where you need to clean house.

The habit of setting up boundaries in relationships is crucial to your emotional and even physical health. There may be some negative people in your life that, for a time, you will not be able to answer their phone calls or continue on those lunch dates. And yes, you must also discipline yourself to not seek out those you feel really comfortable complaining to because you know they will validate you as a victim.

There also may be some hard conversations that need to take place. Do not be a person who shies away from hard conversations. I am not telling you to start telling everyone "what's up," or to be like a bull in a china closet. I am just saying there are possibly some people in your life that you need to sit down with and, in love, share the changes you are making regarding no more gossip, negativity, doubt, or "poor me" attitudes, and that you need their support. I have found when I share my journey and what I am going through and doing for myself, that it disarms people. Who knows? You might be just what they need to make a change in their own life as well.

When you start respecting yourself, others will follow suit and respect you, too.

Taking it a step further, some of you need to hear this: No one should be allowed to physically, sexually, or emotionally harm you. There is a saying that goes like this; "Abuse me once, shame on you. Abuse me twice, shame on me."

If you allow others to abuse you emotionally, sexually, or physically, you are being a partner to their abuse. Share your new journey with them (if feasible), draw your line in love, and most importantly, pray for them. You are not a bad person by separating yourself with boundaries from people who do not and will not respect and value you.

When we talk about boundaries and our gates, I cannot forget to mention the music we listen to, the movies, television and Internet programs we watch, and the books we read. What we are programmed by is what we allow to enter through our gates. Anything that comes through the gates and takes you back to the old negative thoughts, or tempts you to compromise your priorities, needs a boundary.

Once again, not an easy process; but, you will thank yourself one day soon. I would rather walk alone for a while than be with someone that brings a toxic atmosphere into my gates. I would rather cancel my television services and sit in silence than watch something that sends a message contrary to what I want for my life. I would rather throw a book away than take my imagination to places that could cause damage to my marriage, or program things contrary to my new truths.

In these first 63 days, people should not be allowed in your inner circle unless they speak life and are headed in the same direction. There are special circumstances when the toxic person may be in your home and you cannot necessarily get away. If you are married to the person, or they live in your home and will not honor your requests, then please seek counsel. Counseling is not a taboo. I dare to say we ALL need it at times in our lives. I am definitely a fan of life coaches and counselors!

Personal Notes and Insights

_____

_____

_____

_____

_____

_____

_____

_____

_____

_____

_____

_____

_____

_____

_____

_____

_____

_____

_____

_____

_____

Chapter 8

Forgiveness and Failure

What is Forgiveness?

1. Forgiveness is letting God take care of justice. God is our vindicator!

2. Forgiveness is a process. It takes time when something hurts so deeply. Sometimes, the emotions need to be acknowledged and not pushed down before we can forgive.

3. Forgiveness is not an option. I am a Christian and, from my beliefs, I know Christ freely forgave me and expects me to forgive others, too. Even if you are not a believer in Christ, please know that forgiveness is not an option for you. Unforgiveness only holds you in bondage.

4. Forgiveness has to be given even when the person does not ask for it.

5. Forgiveness is a choice. It is a mental decision that our emotions will have to line up with. Sometimes, this is a process that we have to work through. If you have forgiven someone and months later have bitter feelings of resentment towards them, you just stop, tell yourself you have forgiven them, and remind yourself how important forgiveness is to your health.

> "LET NO MAN PULL YOU LOW ENOUGH
>
> TO HATE HIM."
>
> ~MARTIN LUTHER KING JR.

As we are on our journey to wholeness and loving ourselves, forgiveness and failure are two topics that have to be addressed. Let's look at failure. We must come to the understanding that we ALL fail and will continue to fail at times until the end of our lives. It is important to realize that failure is not our identity; it is only our results that sometimes fail. In that moment of failure, what we learn, and how we deal with failure, is crucial to what we become. How we deal with failure will determine our future growth and wholeness.

I can remember times in the past when I would fail and beat myself up so badly. The failure was like a slide show that was set on repeat. Self-sabotaging led to the building of more negative thoughts because I could not forgive myself for failing. Little did I know that embracing failure could be my friend. It could be a tool that sharpened me, it could be a teacher that schooled me on how to rise up and learn from this mistake. According to John Maxwell, "Sometimes we win, sometimes we learn." Oh, how I wish earlier in my life that someone could have convinced me to fail forward; that with each failure I could be made stronger. To embrace it, learn, and then to get back up. My friends, life is forward motion. It is meant to be lived looking out the front windshield, not the rear-view mirror! We call what is in the rear-view mirror "road kill." The past can be learned from, but not focused on, or a place we live from.

Isn't it crazy how easy it is to live in the failures of the past and carry around unforgiveness towards ourselves? We feel like we must make ourselves pay for our wrongs. You know, that tendency we all have, to indulge our own guilt. It is sometimes easier to complain than to get up and make a change. Decide to acknowledge your mistake, embrace and learn from it, make needed changes, and move forward. Forgive yourself of yesterday's failure and allow it to be a catalyst for tomorrow's change.

> "YOUR ATTITUDE TOWARDS FAILURE DETERMINES YOUR ALTITUDE AFTER FAILURE." ~JOHN MAXWELL

ACTIVATION

Ten easy steps to help you forgive yourself:

1. Identify the mistake.

2. Share with a trusted friend for support. This lets others see that no one is perfect and we all make mistakes. Plus, it helps you with number 3.

3. Identify any unrealistic expectations you may have put on yourself. *For example:* Your mother had a stroke and you did not move her into your home. You cannot forgive yourself. You hear a negative voice that says, "Everyone moves their mother in, right?" But, your mother is very critical, bitter, negative, and to move her in would negatively affect everyone in your home. Sharing this with someone can help you see that you have put unrealistic expectations on yourself. It is ok to protect yourself and your family and move your mother into assisted living.

4. Identify the hurt, guilt, and stress you feel from unforgiveness. These feelings are damaging your physical body, how they are affecting the way you perceive life, and the way you interact with those you love.

5. Apologize to yourself, God, and anyone else if needed. Then, visually see yourself receiving the forgiveness.

6. Stop the replay of the event. Every time you catch yourself watching the reenactment of your failure or what you might see as a sin, stop, throw it in your mind's eye trash can, and refocus on something more positive.

7. What have you learned from the mistake, and how can you make it right? Are you beating yourself up for not being the parent you needed to be? You might not be able to change the past, but you can be an amazing grandparent! You can pour into other kids around you. Fred Luskin, Ph.D. and Director of Stanford University specializes in forgiveness and says, "Do good, rather than feel bad."

8. Do not identify yourself with the failure, or sin. Add to your affirmations if needed, and tell yourself the new truth of who you are.

9. Focus on the things you have done right, and on your strengths and gifting. When you do this, you will realize how amazing you truly are!

10. Practice gratitude. Keep a gratitude journal of all the things you are thankful and grateful for. Gratitude changes your perception.

So many times, we take on failure as our identity. Just because we fail at something does not mean we have to wear the name tag of, "I'm a failure." If we learn from it, the failure could be the tool that boosts us on to our success. Wearing the name tag of failure is a lie that is trying to form in your mind and build a stronghold; a wall. Throw it away and replace it with, "I learn from my failures and I get back up. I forgive myself quickly."

Are you allowing past failures to hold you in bondage?

When I was younger, I did not possess the tools to be a good friend. One time in particular I broke a confidence with someone that was close to me in my life and shared something she told me confidentially. I was so broken from my failure and the hurt it caused my dear friend. I started to tell myself that I was a horrible friend, did not have what it took to be good at friendship, and that I was a failure in this area. That was what put me in bondage and built walls between me and others. For years, I would not let people get close to me because I was a "failure at friendship." Later in life, during my healing process, I had to forgive myself. I even asked forgiveness from my friend. I learned from this that true friends keep confidentiality, and how hurtful breaking confidentiality can be. I started confessing over my life that I was a good friend. Today, I am proud to say that friendship is something I am good at. Even though my inner circle is small, I love my friends well, and see the value in confidentiality!

Years ago, I had the desire to be an entrepreneur and bring money into our home. I am so thankful that I was blessed to be a stay-at-home mom when my kids were younger. A common struggle I see with moms that do not work out of the home is that they are often unable to contribute financially to the household. I always wanted to be home but also do something that would provide income.

Someone convinced me to join a Network Marketing Company with hopes of becoming rich. I quickly joined and convinced all my friends and family that this was what we needed to do. It was not long before I found out that this particular company, which is no longer in business, was very hard to be successful in. Not only did I not succeed, but my dear friends and family who spent their hard-earned money and valuable time failed, too.

If you have ever walked through something like this, you can identify with me that it can be traumatic if not dealt with correctly. Not knowing then what I do now about failure, I found myself taking on the guilt. I felt guilty not only for my own failures, but also my dear family's and friend's failures and swore I would never do Network Marketing again!

I have to laugh now and remind myself NEVER to say NEVER! For a while I avoided the people I convinced to join because of my own guilt and shame. This was about the same time I had failed in my friendship so you can guess what a basket case I was. I was a failure at friendship and now a failure in business. I was in bondage to this for years because I did not get up, learn, and forgive myself quickly. I did not have the tools I have now. Finding my identity in my failures robbed me of years of joy!

Luckily, I was able to deal with this in my healing process. Years later I joined another Network Marketing company, and had great success. What about you? Are you allowing past failures to hold you in bondage? This may have opened up another area that you need to spend some time on and create new truths to speak over your life. "I make good decisions. I am wise. I am successful in business. I am a good friend!"

These are just a few of my stories. I have failed many times in my life, in so many different areas. But know this, my failure of the past neither defines me, nor my future. I have forgiven myself, and asked God to forgive me and to give me wisdom. Now, I will purpose to use failure as stepping stones, not stumbling blocks!

Areas that we have failed in and take on as guilt are broad: from betraying a friend, to having an affair; from struggling in business, to yelling at our kids, eating a donut, missing days at the gym, skipping our affirmations, to having an abortion. The 10-step formula I shared with you will help you start your journey of freedom from this imprisonment. Acknowledge your mistake, ask for forgiveness, learn what needs to be adjusted to be successful in this area, forgive yourself, confess the truth, and continue on living life with gratitude and in a forward motion.

As you become a strong, confident person that quickly forgives themselves and embraces failure as a learning experience, your children will follow suit. You are leaving a legacy that will be passed on for generations to come.

> "FAILURE IS ANOTHER STEPPING STONE
>
> TO GREATNESS." – OPRAH WINFREY

Forgiving Others

Now that we have learned about forgiving ourselves, let's take a look at forgiving others. I want to start this section with mentioning what forgiveness of others is not:

1. Forgiving someone does not mean that what they did was permissible. Learn to separate the person from the hurtful act.

2. Forgiving someone does not mean you have to be friends with them.

3. Forgiving someone does not mean you are to let the offense happen again and again. Setting boundaries is healthy.

4. Forgiveness is not reconciliation.

5. Forgiveness is not based on someone having to apologize.

6. The person does not always have to know we forgave them.

7. Forgiveness does not mean forgetting. You may never forget the act, but forgiving the person sets you free to start your inner healing process. You have the ability to remember something without the memory continuing to hurt, just like a scar no longer stings.

Let's take a look at Mary and John again. When Mary and John were ready to start their journey to freedom, they realized they had to forgive their peers, the men that invaded and violated them, and also forgive their fathers. They did not know where to start, so they each sought out the advice of a friend that they could safely confide in. Each of their friends convinced Mary and John to get help. Their friends knew great counselors and also helped set up their appointments. In these counseling sessions, they were both able to not only express all the hurt in their lives, but confide of their desire not to be held in bondage anymore.

Sometimes in life your unforgiveness is from events that happened long ago. In this instance, you will not always be able to find those people that are responsible for your hurt and, furthermore, may no longer even have any desire to find them.

Let It Go!

Mary and John both realized that holding unforgiveness towards their peers was not hurting their peers, but was only hurting them. Their bitterness was negatively affecting them personally, as well as affecting their children and their marriages. They made the decision to release their peers, and forgive their rejection and hurtful words. Mary and John sat in their respective living rooms alone one day, spoke to their peers as though their peers were sitting in the living room with them, and told them they were forgiven. When this happened, Mary and John had new-found strong feelings of compassion for their peers, and each realized these people must have been hurt themselves to become so mean.

> ## "HURT PEOPLE HURT PEOPLE."
>
> ### – BILL BOWEN.

Mary and John both had also lived their life thinking their sexual abuse was their own fault. They blamed themselves. They had nothing solid to base this on, but just automatically felt guilt and shame. Neither Mary nor John ever told anyone what had happened and constantly pushed the memories and feelings away. These memories only brought dark guilt and shame. On Mary's and John's journey to wholeness, both discovered how important it was to bring all their feelings to the surface and acknowledge them. Through not pushing the feelings away and being able to share them in a safe place, Mary and John could acknowledge what happened to them. Their perception suddenly changed as they shared these hurtful events. It was like someone turned the light on and brought clarity to the situation. They realized it was not their fault and, through this process, knew they had to forgive themselves for the guilt they felt. Suddenly, they could think clearly. They also realized that, by forgiving the men who abused them, Mary and John would be set free from the chains that bound them.

Mary's and John's fathers were both still alive at the time of their revelation on forgiveness. They both felt they needed to let their fathers know that they were forgiven. The relationship they had with their fathers had been estranged for years. Mary and John met their fathers in a coffee shop and told them of their emotional healing journey. They also told them of how their negative words had affected them so much, and how they grew to resent them; thus, the reason their relationship was strained and distant. Mary and John looked their fathers in the eyes, and each told their father they forgave them. They each knew their father was hurt on the inside from stories they heard about their father's own emotionally abusive mother. Mary and John both said, "It stops here." They told their fathers that hurt people hurt people, and how easy it was to carry this on from generation to generation. Mary's and John's fathers were broken, shed tears, and even asked for forgiveness. They were able to lead their fathers through forgiving their own abusive parents and starting their own healing journey, too.

They will tell you that all their healing (especially from sexual abuse) did not happen overnight, but rather was a process to work through. Mary and John were both Christians and found great healing in taking their memories and emotions to Jesus and allowing Him to heal them. Several people are credited for helping

Mary and John forgive and start their healing journey. They credit themselves, a trusted friend, a counselor, and Jesus Christ.

Not always do our stories of forgiveness go like this. Sometimes, when you tell someone that you have forgiven them, they become defensive, mad, or deeply hurt. This is why it is always good to pray and give much thought to whether or not you need to share the forgiveness process with them, or simply keep it to yourself. Forgiveness is more about you than it is with them. It is not letting something that brings so much pain control you anymore. Go with your intuition, your gut feeling, listen to that still soft voice inside of you and, if you feel this will bring restoration or healing to you or the one that you are forgiving, then by all means, share your feelings with them openly. However, if you realize you will not be able to handle it well if they do not respond in the way you are hoping they will, it is best not to seek a personal encounter with them.

Sexual abuse happens to boys and girls, and men and women alike. Many men have been sexually assaulted as young boys; many women as young girls. I want you to know you are not alone in your silent suffering. I beg you, please do not live in your pain. Confide in someone that specializes in helping others heal due to sexual abuse. It may be a counselor, a pastor, or someone trained in emotional healing. If you were the victim of sexual abuse, you are not alone.

Chapter 9

Living to Leave a Legacy

In my workshop, "Living to Leave a Legacy," part of the day is spent on dealing with offense. This has proven to be one of the most powerful sessions in the day thus far. Testimonies always flood in on how people's lives were changed from this powerful topic. So many have no idea they were holding offense towards others. In the workshop, I teach how to let go of past offense, and live a life where you are not offended.

If you find yourself having to forgive others on a constant basis, it is a good idea to ask yourself if you are easily offended.

The Greek word for offense is *skandalizo*, which means a stumbling block, to trip up, or entrap.

The Banana Trap

Little monkeys are worth a lot of money but are hard to capture. Trappers have discovered a weakness in these cute little creatures; they love bananas. So much so, that when they find a banana, they will not let go of it.

The trapper finds a coconut and drills a hole big enough to put a banana in. He then chains the coconut to a tree and places bananas around the coconut. One special banana goes on the inside of the coconut. He knows that when the monkeys swing through the trees, they will see the bananas. He also knows one of those cute little monkeys will spot the banana inside the coconut and will be tempted to reach his hand into the coconut and grasp the banana.

The trapper is wise to know the monkey's vice. He knows the desire the monkey has for the banana and that the monkey's clinched fist will not allow him to pull his hand out. Even though he cannot remove his clinched fist from the coconut, he refuses to release the banana and becomes entrapped. The monkey will thrash all night trying to get the banana out and will be exhausted the next morning. So exhausted, in fact, that it is a piece of cake for the trapper to pick him up and put him in a cage. The banana becomes the bait which entraps the monkey just as holding onto offense keeps you and me in bondage.

There is a war going on right now for your freedom and your destiny. So much so that traps have been set to lure you off track. I am hoping this section of the book clearly reveals one of those traps. My goal is to bring an awareness to you that:

1. Holding onto offense will hold you in bondage and

2. That you can live a life free from offense.

So many are caught up in this sneaky trap of offense. Many have clinched onto the banana and are chained to the tree. This trap is keeping so many people busy thrashing around that they are missing their destiny. Little do they know that all they have to do is open their hand and let go.

What about you? Are you wearing your feelings on your shoulders and constantly getting them hurt? Do you struggle with feelings of woundedness, revenge, and bitterness? What about judgment? Do you constantly feel left out? Aren't you sick of it? I know there was a time in my own life where I was sick and tired of the strife and drama; tired of the feelings of self-pity. When the curtains were finally pulled back and I saw clearly what was happening, I was so disappointed to see I had been tricked and was holding on with a clinched fist to a rotten banana of offense.

When I realized offense was one of the reasons for my misery, I began to wonder why I was getting easily offended? I knew I had to stop being offended, but I couldn't. This led me to my journey on finding out the root of the issue. This root will leave a door cracked open for the lies to come in. I had to get that door shut. I came up with several reasons that opened the door in my own life for offense. Let's take a minute and examine each one.

Four reasons that most commonly cause us to be offended:

1. Insecurity

2. Jealousy

3. Selfishness

4. Unrealistic expectations

1. Insecurity:

Earlier in life, I was in an identity crisis of not knowing who I was. This crisis caused great insecurity. Not knowing who I was caused me to be consumed about my inadequacies, my hurt feelings, and worries of everyone liking me. I did not know that a confident woman of virtue was on the inside and ready to come out. I just felt insecurity, and one of the things insecurity did was lure me into the trap of comparison. Comparison is very dangerous to our true identity. It is so dangerous that I think we need to take time out and look at the dangers of comparison.

When we are insecure we compare ourselves to others which causes us to:

a. Conform

b. Become jealous

c. Be paralyzed.

Before we move on, let's take a closer look at each one of these.

a. Comparison Causes Us to Conform

When we compare ourselves to others, we will conform into something we were not created to be. An example of that could be an insecure mother who works outside of her home, starts looking around at other moms, and compares her life with theirs. She says to herself, "They are stay-at-home moms. It seems like their kids are amazing. I wonder if that is what I should do?"

b. Comparison Causes Jealousy

When we compare, we become jealous and therefore very critical. Consider a businessman who is struggling and compares himself to a very successful man in town. He becomes very jealous of the businessman's success and finds himself looking for faults in the other man. The successful businessman tells him, "You have to come play golf with us during the week. You are missing out." The struggling man is offended because he has to work, is trying to make ends meet, and cannot leave. He begins to think the successful man was just taunting him because he knew he probably would not be able to leave. This leads the struggling man to say of the successful businessman, "He never spends quality time with his family. His success was handed to him. He really has no talent. He is so full of himself. Doesn't he know pride comes before a fall?" The successful businessman just wanted to include him in social activities. The struggling man does not truly know the successful man's heart or what his life really looks like behind closed doors.

c. Comparison Causes Us to Become Paralyzed

When we compare ourselves with others, we can become paralyzed and adopt a "why even try" attitude. Conformity can lead us to feeling either superior, or inferior. Both of these are dangerous because they will keep us away from being confident in who we are. Our goal needs to be humility. One of my very favorite quotes on this is by Mother Teresa who said, "If you are humble, nothing will touch you, neither praise nor disgrace, because you know what you are."

As we just discovered, one reason you and I are easily offended is because of insecurity. Let's look at the other three reasons why we are easily offended:

2. Selfishness

Being constantly consumed about ourselves produces self-ishness. "Why did they look at me like that? He never even said thank you. I wasn't even invited. Me, Myself and I." Yuck!! Once I started to see my selfishness for what it was, I became disgusted by this victim mentality and selfishness. This plays right into our next reason.

3. Past Experiences

In my earlier years, I found that I focused a lot on my past. Yesterday's problems and hurts kept the past in the present and caused me to filter everyone else's words and actions through them. Rejection from the past caused me to perceive that others were always rejecting me and I would easily get offended with them. For example, when they did not agree with me, did not speak to me, or show interest in me or my ideas; when they turned down an invitation, or simply did not return my calls. All of these things caused me to feel rejected and get offended. When we behave this way, others do not want to be around us because they feel as though they have to walk on egg shells. Do not perceive people today through yesterday's experiences.

Have you had a marriage or serious relationship of infidelity, maybe a parent that manipulated you with control? If so, I would say you might be viewing your present relationships through those experiences. It is not fair to view others who want to love you today through the lens of those that hurt you yesterday.

You can probably see where unhealed past experiences can definitely cause offense.

4. Unrealistic Expectations

So many times in life we put unrealistic expectations on others. Usually this happens when we have inner turmoil from being too hard on ourselves. It comes out in the form of being hard on others around us. I see this a lot in parents and coaches that are much too hard on their kids. I can clearly remember a time in my life of not liking who I was and being disappointed in myself. It was in those years that I expected perfection in others and viewed their results and actions critically through a magnifying glass. When my first son was very small, I saw that he was athletically gifted. My husband and I teamed up to rope steers in rodeo competitons and we recognized that our son was also going to be very talented with his hands. One day as I was teaching him to rope the plastic horns in a bale of hay, my husband pointed out that I was expecting too much. I will never forget his words, "Kelly, some people nudge their kids. You push yours off a cliff." Wow! I am very thankful for my emotional and spiritual healing that took place in my early years. It allowed me to parent in a way that was healthy and not have unrealistic expectants on my children. Today, my son rodeos at a professional level, but it was totally by his choice and not because his parents pushed him or tried to live their life through him.

A great example that will probably hit home is with your spouse. Do you expect them to know what you need without ever telling them; from taking out the trash, to needing more quality time? Do not expect them to just know or read your mind. That is unrealistic and can cause you to be offended.

Receiving grace from God, and myself, allowed me to give it freely and easily to people around me whom I loved dearly.

Some examples of unrealistic expectations might include expecting others to apologize first, or to know our needs without telling them; expecting everyone to like you, or thinking you can change another person; thinking you will never fail, or expecting perfection from yourself and others. These are just a few areas of unrealistic expectations that can lead to disappointment and result in taking offense.

Once I realized what was happening, I became disgusted with these little traps and tired of the turmoil offense was keeping me in. This little fox of offense always brought his cousins with him, too: bitterness, strife, anger, gossip, resentment. Offense never travels alone!

In summary, insecurity, past experiences, selfishness and unrealistic expectations are four reasons why you and I get easily offended.

All of this information is great for awareness and evaluation, but if we do not apply these next principles, we will stay in the pit of offense.

Releasing Offense

Mary and John were both deeply offended with their fathers. Their abusive words of the past caused them to hold feelings of bitterness, hatred, and disgust toward their parents. As we saw earlier, when Mary and John were in counseling, they discovered they had to let go of the offense and forgive their fathers. Their counselors told them to start praying for their fathers. Not a prayer that they would be struck by lightning, but a prayer of blessing. They were told to pray a prayer like they wished someone would pray for them. Their counselors also suggested they ask God to give them a supernatural love for their fathers; the love that God had for their fathers. These two things are what sparked Mary and John to meet their fathers in the coffee shop and forgive them.

What about you? Are there people in your life that you hold offense toward? You know, when you see them you feel annoyed and have a grudge? Is there anyone in your life that you secretly hope will fail; you are disappointed when you hear they are successful, or have received a blessing? Who do you find yourself talking about and reliving what they have done to you? If anyone comes to mind, these are people that you are holding offense toward. Take time to open your hand and release the offense. Pray for them, bless them, do random acts of kindness towards them, and you will start to feel a sense of freedom!

Note: Offense likes to hide, and many times we have no idea that we are holding on to it.

Creating an Atmosphere Free of Offense

This is the chapter we have all been waiting for; how to live a life and never take offense. You may wonder how in the world one gets to a place where you no longer get offended? I believe you can live a life free of offense. You can be a man or woman that cannot be offended!

This kind of life starts with speaking your affirmations daily. When you speak your affirmations daily and change your toxic thought patterns, a sense of peace starts to form and you begin to see yourself as valuable; you begin to love yourself again. Other people's actions or opinions do not affect you so greatly.

When you decide to choose love, it is easier to let things go. Choosing love gives grace. I once heard that hate is just the absence of love.

Another practice is to celebrate others. Creating a habit of celebrating others verbally on the spot, or by sending a text message or card, creates an atmosphere where jealousy has to leave.

As we are creating this offense-free atmosphere, we cannot forget to let go of perfection and remember that no one's actions are perfect 100% of the time. We are all in need of grace, and we all need to know it is alright to fail, and that we can learn from it. Remember, hurt people, hurt people, as Bill Bowen would put it. If we all wore sticky notes of the current struggles we were going through, then, we would see each other's scars. When someone hurts you, let that be a realization to you that they are also hurting. This will cause you to have compassion for them rather than take offense.

The most powerful habit I have started is what I like to call the 10-second rule. The 10-second rule is based on the fact that your mind has about 10 seconds to hold on to something and either imprint it, or release it. Those 10 seconds after you start to feel offense (because we all do) are crucial. When you feel that slight irritation, annoyance, hurt feelings, comparison, not being included, feeling threatened or mistreated, is when you stop, capture that thought or feeling, and say to yourself, "I will not be offended. I am letting this go." Then, picture yourself throwing it away in your mind's eye trash can. As you start to practice this, it will become a habit. You will automatically enlist the 10 second rule when someone cuts you off in traffic, when your spouse, friend or loved one hurts your feelings, or makes you mad. If you will apply this, I promise you it will work!

Offense often occurs because we do not know all the details (there is usually a bigger picture) or, we are perceiving through our filters of past hurt.

As you can see, offense is a vast topic. So far you have learned:

1. Offense is a trap.

2. Offense holds you in bondage and weighs you down.

3. There are four major areas that can cause you to be offended.

4. How to let go of offense.

5. How to live a life not offended.

If you can make a habit to apply these principles in your life, your heart and mind will start to become fertile soil where you can plant seeds to dream again. Instead of dragging a ball and chain, you will feel ready to take flight.

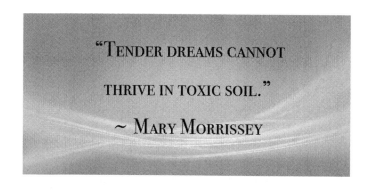

"TENDER DREAMS CANNOT

THRIVE IN TOXIC SOIL."

~ MARY MORRISSEY

Fulfilling Your Purpose

When I was little, I dreamed of being a movie star. Don't laugh. It's true! At only four or five years old, my family would be sitting in the living room watching TV and I would announce to them that I would be on TV one day. Years later, my talents and passions came out in community theater and competitive speaking. The one and only semester that I attended college I was cast in a role in our college play. I was going to major in mass communications and do something big in front of a camera. My poor choices found me flunking out of school, broke, and heading back home to live with my parents in the small trailer house I grew up in. I was a broken young woman with big dreams that had been shattered.

I came back home from college Christmas of 1993 and met my husband just a few months later. We married a year and a half later and my journey of emotional healing began. In 1997, we had our son, Brady. He was our first child together. We soon decided that the right thing for our young family was for me to not work outside of the home. Everyone has to do what is right for them, and for us it was me staying home.

Looking back, I know we made the right choice for myself and our family. Actually, I consider those early years some of the best times of my life. I spent most of my time washing clothes, cleaning the house, feeding my family, which could be considered a full-time job, and reading the Bible. I discovered the love of God in those pages. He taught me to pour my heart out to Him and let Him heal it. This is when I discovered affirmations and began to declare the truth over my life. Most of the things I have written about in this book I learned in those wonderful years.

Our boys were six years apart so this time at home stretched out for several years. I loved staying home. I loved cooking for my family and taking care of them. I loved getting to know who God really was. Experiencing the love He had for me was so healing. I knew when my children were born that one of my greatest callings in life was to raise godly men; men that had compassion for others, kindness, wisdom, courage, confidence, strength, and most of all, a love for God.

I remember one day, as I was making the bed and pulling those fitted sheets over the ends, hearing a still soft voice speak within me say, "You will speak to many." I paused and wondered, was that my imagination playing a trick on me? Was that from my own desires and dreams I had as a child? Or, could God be speaking to me?

I lived in a town with a population of 700 people. Most of my days consisted of life on our small ranch raising boys, with the highlights being weekly trips to Walmart, church, and taking our oldest son to junior rodeos. I was just a small-town girl raising boys and cooking chicken-fried steak! Not long after that I was mopping the floor and heard the same still soft voice again. "I have great things in store for your life." I would have dreams of being on a stage, holding a microphone, speaking to crowded rooms. Then, God brought several people into my life who prophetically confirmed that I would speak to many. I would teach and empower others in a simple way that they could hear and understand. I would share my story.

I even received the same Scripture from different people which was from Habakkuk 2:2-3:

Write the vision; make it plain on tablets, so he may run who reads it. For still the vision awaits its appointed time; it hastens to the end—it will not lie. If it seems slow, wait for it; it will surely come; it will not delay.

Do you know how hard it is to receive a dream, a call, a desire before its time?

This leads me to talk to you about your purpose. I believe before you were born you had a specific purpose created just for you. You are one-of-a-kind, a masterpiece sculpted from God. He uniquely and perfectly created you with certain talents, strengths, and desires that would be needed to fulfill that one-of-a-kind purpose for your life. Looking back now, my love for the theatre and speaking were placed in me to fulfill my purpose.

John Maxwell says the beginning of success is "knowing your purpose in life."

But, the hard truth is, we must spend a lot of time before we discover our purpose. Time in prayer and reflection, time trying new things and making new connections. Even time gaining resources and education. But do not let that stop you. Our life is so much about discovering our purpose so that we can not only fulfill it but, most importantly, use it to benefit others.

Three steps to help you find your purpose:

1. Pray

If God uniquely created you, then why in the world would we not ask Him? In Jeremiah 29:11, God tells young discouraged Jeremiah, "I know the plans I have for you, plans to prosper you and not to harm you, plans to give you hope and a future"

(NKJV). If prayer has not been a regular part of your life, then start today. This is the first day of the rest of your life! You are right where you need to be, and God has a plan for you. When you pray, bring a journal and write down anything you are feeling during your prayer time. Prayer is not only us talking, but is a continual cycle of us talking, us listening while God talks, then us talking again, listening again, and on and on. A prayer journal is important to me because I need to go back and remember the things God spoke to me long after the feeling leaves. So many times, I felt great faith in prayer and in receiving what God said to me. Reading what I wrote down in my time with the Lord encourages me and stirs my faith.

2. Strengths, Giftings, Talents, Desires

I am a huge fan of personality testing. You can never learn enough about yourself. There are several free online tests you can take. I also suggest asking yourself a lot of questions.

- What do I love?
- What am I good at?
- What people groups move me with passion and compassion? For example: children, men, women, elderly, fathers, mothers, specific ethnic groups, people with certain struggles, etc.

Most times these answers are clues to your purpose.

3. Step out

Your purpose does not knock on the door and chase you down while you are sitting on the couch eating Cheetos. You cannot think your way into your purpose. Move towards some goals, and try new things. It is then that you will discover what you are and are not made to do.

I now know I am not the woman to call to cook a casserole for a funeral or watch the kids in the nursery. I am not the organizer, decorator, or the homeroom mom. I am not called to bake the beautiful cupcakes. But, I can come and speak to your classroom or organization with only 30 minutes notice, or drop everything and write something with creativity and insight that will move you to think differently! It has taken me courageously trying many things to figure out my purpose. Most of those things consisted of failure; but, in the failure, I learned. It propelled me a step closer to my purpose.

My friends, I do not know exactly what your purpose is or where your purpose lies, but I do know:

1. It is good and

2. You will not find it in your comfort zone. Do not worry. God is a master at rerouting us to get us where He created us to be!

Significance

As I listened to John Maxwell talk about success and finding your purpose, it made my insides stand to attention. He said success is not truly complete without significance. Many people think they have arrived when they find their purpose. Many soon wonder why they are so unhappy after they have discovered the treasure they have been looking for.

I believe the answer to this is found by understanding significance. Significance is obtained when you and I add value to others through our life's purpose; when we understand that the gift was not for us, but rather entrusted to us to be given away. It is then, and only then, that success is complete and we are living a life of significance.

Legacy

My favorite word in this season is legacy. Legacy is when you continue to live and make a difference far after you have died. A legacy is left when we:

1. Know our identity of virtue and valor

2. Have a healthy mindset

3. Forgive

4. Let go of offense

5. Live a life not holding onto offense

6. Discover our purpose and add value to others through it

Do you want to impact your great, great, grandchildren's lives?

Do you want to change the world around you for generations to come?

If you answered yes, then let that compel you to apply the principles you are learning through this book. Let them become a habit that you live by the rest of your life.

Personal Notes and Insights

_____

_____

_____

_____

_____

_____

_____

_____

_____

_____

_____

_____

_____

_____

_____

_____

_____

_____

_____

_____

_____

_____

_____

Conclusion

Destination Freedom

We've taken this journey together and have covered much ground. Our travels from the introduction to the conclusion of this book have mapped the way for you to rise up from the lowest ground of defeat, to the apex of the mountain of self-worth. As your destination began to come into view, the course of events leading up to that point began to move from the forefront of the image in the mirror that reflected the loss of hope, to the point where your new promise-filled destiny is now able to replace your history, and your legacy is based more on your tomorrow than your yesterday.

You cannot change your past, but you can certainly rewrite it. You can now bring a new and fresh perspective to the events that shaped your life so that your image in the mirror reflects you as the person with the potential to realize your own greatness, craft an exciting future, and re-fire those dreams you thought were nothing more than smoldering embers.

The John from our story no longer has a toy sword. He has now been reinvigorated, his strength has returned, and his sword is one of confidence in his ability to conquer the unconquerable. Our Mary no longer walks around in heels that are too big for her and play princess dresses. Her new clothes not only fit perfectly, but blend in beautifully with a lifestyle that now exemplifies personal promise, great expectation, and dreams fulfilled.

Just like Mary and John, your own reflection in the mirror has changed drastically. You now hold the blueprint for continued success and unrivaled personal growth, your future has the capacity to look as bright as you choose to see it, your life now coincides with the image in your mirror, and you are loving what, and who, you see!

About

Kelly Norman

Kelly Norman is a wife, mother, certified John Maxwell speaker, trainer, coach and a successful entrepreneur. Early in her life, she felt insecure and imprisoned within her own mind. Tormented by destructive thought patterns, Kelly knew there had to be more to life!

In 1998, Kelly began her journey towards what she calls FREEDOM. Her success in overcoming her own adversities and finding freedom and confidence in who she was created to be, stirred within her a desire to help others. Success in the business world offered Kelly a platform to speak to people across the United States.

"My success as an entrepreneur is allowing me to fulfill my life-long dream of sharing my story and life lessons that led me to my freedom. I hope to awaken, inspire and empower others to live a life of FREEDOM and to leave a legacy."

Kelly is now speaking to audiences across the country about how to truly love themselves and discover their unique and divine purpose to change the world around them.

Kelly speaks on topics such as identity, success, mindset, dreaming, leadership, overcoming offense and so much more. Many lives will be awakened and empowered to walk in freedom because Kelly chose to share her story.

Look for a "Legacy" workshop near you!

www.kellyjnorman.com

Kelly J. Norman

P O Box 82

Springer, OK 73458

Testimonials

I had the privilege of hosting Kelly Norman's "Living a Legacy" workshop and, to say it changed the way I look at life, is an understatement. Never having hosted an event, I was somewhat nervous about its logistics and promotion. Kelly's calmness and easy demeanor quickly removed my worries. She helped me make it seamless, simple, and enjoyable.

I went into the event thinking, "I'm sure I've heard most of this before." Was I wrong. Kelly's lessons on dealing with offense were something I had never heard before. I left with tools that I knew I needed to apply to my life. The way she intertwined her life and stories made her relatable and real, vulnerable and raw, which is not something you see often.

Months later, I still carry those lessons and apply them daily. But, more importantly, Kelly has become a friend, mentor, and someone I love so much. It is clear she was put on this earth for a purpose; to bring out greatness in people they do not even know they have; to provide tools that people do not even know exist; to pour love and belief into people so that they can all live better lives. I am forever grateful for our friendship.

Erin O'Keefe

Each year I pick one word for the year that I believe God wants to build in me and through me. This year the word was 'obey.' I have learned that it is because of God's faithfulness that I, too, can be faithful and obey God more effectively.

Back track to 2014. That was the very first year I had ever heard about #oneword; my word at that time was FREEDOM. I was separated from my husband because of domestic violence. I needed to be free from that situation but felt like a failure. I beat myself up and carried around baggage from that failed marriage.

I have been divorced for only a short year and a half. I have five children from that failed marriage which left me as a single mother struggling to figure out how I was going to leave a lasting legacy in their lives and raise them up to be warriors on a course to change the world. So, I started college. Again!

I kept pushing into the resistance and pressure that comes from being a single parent. Kelly helped propel me into my God-given destiny. I began watching her videos in the summer of 2016. The love and light she shared about loving myself started a paradigm shift in me. I did not even know what that phrase "paradigm shift" meant until she entered my life.

Kelly has been a divine force in my life. I already have an influence among other women that is strengthened because she empowered me, to empower them. I am eager to watch what Kelly will do next and what they will teach me and so many other women.

Jessie Reagan

I actively participated in two of Kelly's training sessions this past year. One was her monthly mentorship calls, and the other was her online Mastermind from John Maxwell's book *Intentional Living*. I just cannot say enough good things about the benefits I received in just one hour per week with Kelly.

She goes out of her way to personally interact with each member of her group, and it is immediately obvious that she truly cares and takes an active interest in each and every life. With modest finances, I have never had the money to hire a life coach or business coach; but, Kelly came close to filling both of these roles at a mere fraction of the typical cost.

I came away from each session with increased self-confidence and a better vision for what I should be doing next to advance in life. Best of all, I feel like I have gained a life-long friend.

Thank you, Kelly, for enriching my life in such a special way.

Anne-Marie Blevins

I first met Kelly at a corporate training meeting for my company. She made a point of coming right up to me, as well as everyone else, and introducing herself. I had heard from others that I would like her because she was a "straight shooter," but she was so much more than that.

Not many people have the ability to be bold, honest, and speak about very controversial or hot topics while remaining vulnerable, genuine, and inspiring. Kelly does it all! Her story will bring you to tears, her training is life changing, and the way she delivers such motivating ideas and practical tools made me feel like, "I can actually do this!"

In a nutshell, Kelly makes people feel like they CAN overcome anything, beginning with changing the way they think; that you do not have to be bound by your past experiences, and can truly live your wildest dreams. I look forward to attending many more trainings and workshops in the future. I'll take all I can get!

Kristen Wyatt

There are the obvious moments that are life changing: engagements, marriages, births, geographical moves, or new jobs all come readily to mind. But then, there are moments in time that change us in ways we do not anticipate. A cold spring day spent in Kelly's legacy training was one of those defining moments for me.

As a former teacher turned stay-at-home momma, I had gotten very comfortable in my role as mom, and advocate for my children. About 18 months before I attended Kelly's workshop, I started a journey with a social networking company solely to help my oldest daughter get healthy. This completely unexpected journey opened up my mind to the possibility of dreaming with my heart again, and revisiting my love of teaching.

Through the power of social media, I had started following Kelly as a mentor in the areas of both professional and personal convictions. I entered Kelly's workshop only expecting to gain a few business tips, but what I left with was so much more. I left ready to build a legacy I was proud of.

As women, moms, wives, daughters, sisters, and friends, we so often pour into the cups of everyone around us, while neglecting to fill our own. It was a complete blessing that I was able to be home and raise my kids, but in doing so I stopped seeking the things that I was passionate about. The way that Kelly recalled stories from her childhood, and as she grew to be a wife and mother, spoke directly to my heart.

I realized in so many instances I was playing it safe. I was not daring to dream. We want our children to reach for the stars and follow their dreams, but we forget that, instead of just telling them, it is essential to model it for them by chasing the passions that make us whole. We wear so many hats, for so many people, that we forget it is not selfish to have some hats we wear just for us.

Kelly stirred in me the fire to reach my true potential in all areas; to be the best I can be, so I can be better for those around me.

From the first moments of the meeting, until the very last, passion flows through her words. But, the mark of a true leader is that it is not over when the meeting has ended. She continued to pour into us with calls, e-mails, and messages. I am so thankful for the opportunity to have been in Kelly's training, and for the friendship that has resulted!

Brianne Coolidge

Living to Leave a Legacy takes you from idea to action; from, "I have no idea," to a clear picture, plan, and purpose. Kelly led with passion and positivity as she taught our small group how to live intentionally. Her heart is for everyone to know who they are, and who they were created to be. She asks the right questions and creates conversations that unlock the desires of your heart as well as provide the road map to achieving your dreams. The class culture in Kelly's mastermind groups is intimate and engaging. I am forever grateful for Kelly's leadership, and the group, who are now my close friends.

Angie Tarrant

I wish I could really put into words what is in my heart. I have participated with Kelly in two different mentorship groups, and in each one I gained insight into myself and my struggles. I watched a leader in action, and was able to set new goals and attain them.

Kelly has a heart for leading and teaching women. She knows and understands very well the challenge we face in our daily lives. She has gone through so much, as we all have, and has such a beautiful willingness to be transparent and open in order to help those in her classes grow and stretch, and overcome as she has.

When I first met Kelly, I did not think I could ever call someone like her my friend because she is so beautiful, talented, successful, and impactful. She proved me wrong, showing me that she has a huge heart for people, that her love and friendship is not based on outward appearance or achievement, and that she truly has a servant's heart. She taught me to really accept and love myself, reminded me how harmful comparison can be, and gave me a push or two to step out when I needed it.

To not say Kelly's courses have impacted and changed my life would be doing her a great disservice. The connections I made with like-minded women, the friendships fostered, and the personal growth I found for myself have been such a blessing to me, and my family. I am so thankful I trusted that prompting to give her class a try. It has made such a difference to me!

Krista Greer

Kelly Norman's trainings have been life-changing. Her honesty and vulnerability make her teachings and trainings so accessible and REAL for everyone who attends. Every aspect applies to life and the relationships you have with your spouse, children, siblings, friends, co-workers, and even God. Through her trainings, I have found the courage to share my personal truth with the world. To me, that is priceless. I would not have been able to do that without Kelly's training.

Andreya Drury

There are people who come into your life that change a piece of you inside. They stir something deeply within you, and then make your soul feel connected to itself and others in an entirely new way. That is the epitome of Kelly Norman and everything she does.

Kelly's trainings and seminars speak truth to your heart that compel you to change. Not only does she intimately connect with your fears, insecurities, and shortcomings, but she makes you feel empowered because of them. Then, she teaches you how to use those characteristics with your strengths to personally develop and grow into who you were intended to become.

When you invest in one of her courses, you invest in your mind's ability to be and do more, and there is nothing more valuable than that!

Emily Gibson

After hearing Kelly Norman speak, I knew my life would be changed. Her positivity and love of others along with her own life experiences have molded her into an exceptional speaker and author.

Kelly's direction and focus on personal growth and development, and learning how to set boundaries and be a better human, has made such a difference in my life. I love how she incorporates the scriptures and God into her teachings.

I am so thankful for her knowledge and how she taught me to become a better individual which, in return, has a ripple effect on all of the people around me. I know I can take her simple yet effective teachings into my life and improve my personal life and business exponentially.

Kimberly

Personal Notes and Insights

Personal Notes and Insights

_____

_____

_____

_____

_____

_____

_____

_____

_____

_____

_____

_____

_____

_____

_____

_____

_____

_____

_____

_____

_____

_____

_____

_____

Personal Notes and Insights

Personal Notes and Insights

_____

_____

_____

_____

_____

_____

_____

_____

_____

_____

_____

_____

_____

_____

_____

_____

_____

_____

_____

_____

_____

_____

Personal Notes and Insights

_____

_____

_____

_____

_____

_____

_____

_____

_____

_____

_____

_____

_____

_____

_____

_____

_____

_____

_____

_____

_____

_____

_____

Personal Notes and Insights

_____

_____

_____

_____

_____

_____

_____

_____

_____

_____

_____

_____

_____

_____

_____

_____

_____

_____

_____

_____

_____

_____

_____

Made in the USA
Lexington, KY
26 June 2018